RUBBISH MUNCHERS

OF THE ANIMAL WORLD

by Jody Sullivan Rake

Content Consultant:
David Stephens, PhD
Professor of Ecology, Evolution and Behaviour

Reading Consultant:
Professor Barbara J. Fox

raintree
a Capstone company — publishers for children

Raintree is an imprint of Capstone Global Library Limited, a company incorporated in England and Wales having its registered office at 7 Pilgrim Street, London, EC4V 6LB – Registered company number: 6695582

www.raintree.co.uk
myorders@raintree.co.uk

ISBN 978-1-4062-9175-9
18 17 16 15 14
10 9 8 7 6 5 4 3 2 1

British Library Cataloguing in Publication Data
A full catalogue record for this book is available from the British Library.

Editorial Credits
Abby Colich, editor; Kyle Grenz, designer; Jo Miller, media researcher; Katy LaVigne, production specialist

Photo Credits
Alamy: FLPA, 18-19, Pep Roig, 28; Dreamstime: Lim Liang Jin, 14-15; Glow Images: All Canada Photos/ Bob Gurr, 13, First Light/Thomas Kitchin & Victoria Hurst, 10, Stocktrek Images/Terry Moore, 20-21; Newscom: Minden Pictures/Michael Durham, 6, 8-9; Robert Harding: Okapia/Ingo Arndt, 22-23; Science Source: Nigel Cattlin, 24-25, Tom McHugh, cover; Shutterstock: Sebastian Kaulitzki, 26-27; SuperStock: Biosphoto, 16-17, NaturePL, 4-5

Printed in China by Nordica.
1014/CA21401515

CONTENTS

TALKING RUBBISH

All animals eat to survive. Some animal **diets** are odd. Others are just plain disgusting! Rubbish is a part of many animal diets. These animals have **adapted** to eat the rubbish that humans throw away.

diet what an animal eats
adapt change to fit into a new or different environment

seagull

HUNGRY RATS

Brown rats are the most common rubbish eaters. These rats live anywhere that humans live. Brown rats eat almost anything, but they have a balanced diet. They search through rubbish bins for meat, grains, nuts and fruit.

Fact!

Rats are not fussy eaters, but they do not like stale or spoiled food.

MASKED BANDITS

Raccoons are masked **mammals** that eat almost anything. These wild animals from North America tear through rubbish at night. Raccoons lift bin lids with their long fingers. They search rubbish bins for leftover food.

Fact!

Raccoons aren't fussy, but they are clean. Before eating, they often wash their food in whatever water they can find.

mammal animal with hair or fur that gives birth to young and feeds them milk

THUMBED OPOSSUMS

Opossums look like big rats. But they are actually **marsupials**. Like kangaroos, opossums carry their young in pouches. They have another special body part – thumbs! Thumbs make it easier to sort through rubbish.

> ### Fact!
> Opossums compete with rats and cockroaches for food. Sometimes rats and cockroaches *are* their food!

marsupial mammal that carries its young in a pouch

THE BEAR FACTS

Brown bears usually eat plants and small animals. They are also rubbish eaters. Bears help themselves to food from rubbish bins. If humans have food near by, bears will find it. These big animals need to eat lots of food.

Fact!

Bears have a strong sense of smell. Bears use their sense of smell to lead them to food.

RUBBISH-EATING GOATS

Goats are adventurous eaters. They nose around in rubbish looking for scraps of food. These curious creatures chew on anything that looks tasty. Paper, cardboard and fabric are some of their favourite things to chew.

Fact!
Many people drink goat's milk and eat goat's cheese.

Fact!

Seagulls like living near water. But sometimes they are seen around rubbish tips hundreds of miles from the water.

WHAT A GULL WANTS

If you have been to the coast, you've probably seen seagulls. To these birds, nearly anything is a snack. Seagulls near the coast eat **tide pool** creatures, dead sea animals and human rubbish. Don't leave your beach picnic unguarded. They'll eat your food, too!

tide pool small pool that forms at low tide on rocky beaches

AS THE CROW FLIES

Crows are found all over the world. How did these black birds become so widespread? By being clever eaters. They know where to find a good meal, even in a nearby rubbish bin.

Fact!

Crows are clever birds. Scientists have discovered that crows use tools to reach food.

Fact!
Tiger sharks are the least fussy eaters of all sharks. They eat sea creatures that other sharks won't eat.

RUBBISH BINS OF THE SEA

Tiger sharks have been found with enough rubbish in their stomachs to fill a skip. Bottles, number plates and even a chicken run have been found in their stomachs. That's why these sharks are nicknamed "rubbish bins of the sea".

GIANT RUBBISH EATERS

Coconut crabs live on islands in the Indian Ocean. These giant creatures usually eat fruit and coconuts. But they also love eating leftovers they find in rubbish bins.

RUBBISH FOR ROACHES

Cockroaches enjoy a good diet anywhere humans live. They are often only active at night. Rubbish bins are perfect homes for them. Cockroaches nibble bits of food stuck to the rubbish.

HOORAY FOR BACTERIA!

Bacteria are tiny **organisms** that live everywhere. Some bacteria make you ill. Some bacteria keep you healthy. Bacteria break down food in the rubbish that animals have not eaten.

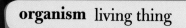

organism living thing

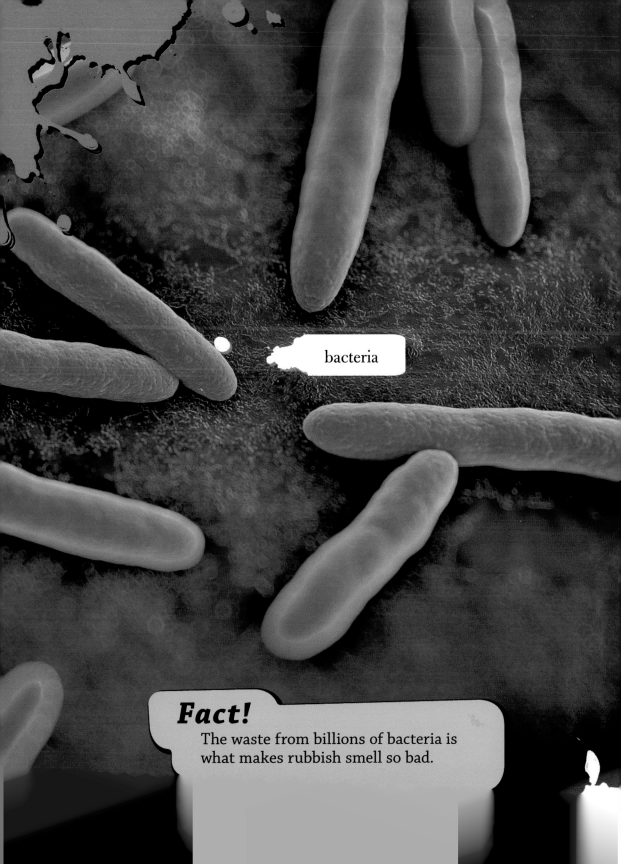

bacteria

Fact!
The waste from billions of bacteria is what makes rubbish smell so bad.

DEADLY DIET

Sometimes eating rubbish is harmful to animals. Animals eat many things in the rubbish that aren't good for them, such as plastic. Eating plastic can make animals ill or even kill them. Always throw away rubbish properly.

Fact!

The best practice for preventing deadly animal diets is to reduce, reuse and recycle!

GLOSSARY

adapt change to fit into a new or different environment

diet what an animal eats

mammal animal with hair or fur that gives birth to young and feeds them milk

marsupial mammal that carries its young in a pouch

organism living thing

tide pool small pool that forms at low tide on rocky beaches

READ MORE

Look Inside a Rubbish Bin (Look Inside a…), Richard and Louise Spilsbury (Raintree, 2014)

Rats (Animal Abilities), Anna Claybourne (Raintree, 2014)

Shark (Eyewitness), Miranda Macquitty (Dorling Kindersley, 2011)

WEBSITES

www.bbc.co.uk/nature/life/Brown_Bear
Watch videos and find out more fascinating facts about these bears and their eating habits.

www.bbc.co.uk/nature/adaptations/Scavenger
Find out more about some of nature's most interesting and inventive scavengers, including life on landfills.

INDEX